DEDICATION

To every woman who's ever been underestimated and still chose to lead.

And to my grandmother, whose strength, vision, and wisdom planted the very seeds that grew this framework.

A MASTERCLASS IN LEADERSHIP

THE 4S

FRAMEWORK

BY

STACIE SELISE™

STACIE SELISE SHANNON

For permissions, licensing, or publishing inquiries, visit www.stacieselise.com.

First Edition | Printed in the United States

ISBN: 979-8-9986995-0-4 (Paperback)

ISBN: 979-8-9986995-1-1 (Hardcover)

A Note from Stacie

I didn't build The 4S Framework because leadership was easy; I built it because I've lived through what it takes to lead with power, grace, and purpose when the odds are stacked against you. From corporate boardrooms to building my own empire, the lessons I learned weren't just about success; they were about alignment, vision, and becoming a force of impact.

This playbook isn't theory. It's a blueprint for becoming the kind of leader who doesn't wait to be chosen. Whether you're leading a team, a business, a classroom, or stepping into leadership for the first time, this is your guide to rise with purpose, presence, and power.

What People Are Saying

"The 4S Framework by Stacie Selise is more than just a leadership guide, it's a blueprint for intentional, impactful leadership. Stacie's real-world experience and transparent storytelling make each pillar—Support, Strive, Standards, and Success—not just concepts, but actionable steps toward elevating your leadership and legacy. As the Founder of NoDefeat Warrior, I deeply resonate with her emphasis on legacy, community impact, and redefining success on your own terms. I wholeheartedly endorse this framework as a transformative tool for leaders who are ready to lead with purpose, presence, and unshakable standards."

—Dr. Shannon Burge
Founder & Executive Director, NoDefeat Warrior
IFBB Pro | Speaker | Executive Coach
www.nodefeat.co | www.nodefeatwarrior.com

"I loved the book. The way Stacie broke down leadership through Support, Strive, Standards, and Success was so clear and relatable. I liked it better than a lot of leadership books I've read because it sounds like someone who's actually done it with real experience.

One thing that really stood out to me was the author's voice. It's rare to read something that feels both motivating and practical, and Stacie nailed it.

Overall, this was a good read. I can see this book being used as a tool during leadership meetings/training!"

—Lily T. Monroe
CEO of ÉLEVÉ Marketing Group

"This book has caused me to question within myself what legacy of leadership I want to be known for. I've been reminded of just why I do what I do, which is all about the people.

When I read about leadership struggles in a male-dominated industry, this deeply resonated with me. As a woman earlier in my career, I was steadily locked out of positions and yet expected to give 110% of myself. I wish I had read and been able to take to heart a book like this back then.

Final Note: This book encourages us as women to feel empowered and valued to the point that we search for a place where we can lead with dignity and strength, and not give up until we find it. This book makes me feel stronger and braver, ready to do what I've always dreamed of, and to never give up. Thank you from the bottom of my heart for writing this, Stacie. I'm so very proud of you. You're truly an inspiration to women of all races and walks of life. I'm honored to know you and have been a small part of this journey with you."

—Amanda Stockton
Chief Client Experience Officer & Executive Career Consultant
The Barrett Group
www.careerchange.com
https://www.linkedin.com/in/amandastockton

Table of Contents

Foreword

've worked alongside a lot of leaders over the years—driven, capable, results-focused. But every now and then, someone stands out, not just for how they perform, but for how they lead. Stacie Selise is one of those people. From the moment we began working together, it was clear she brought more than talent to the table—she brought intention, presence, and a level of emotional intelligence that moved people to follow her.

We worked together across multiple markets during a time of rapid change and rising expectations. I saw firsthand how she leaned into every challenge with clarity, drive, and an undeniable presence. She didn't wait to be told how to lead—she defined leadership on her own terms. Regardless of geography, team makeup, or evolving demands, Stacie always found a way to elevate the people and the culture around her.

What always impressed me most about Stacie wasn't just how she performed under pressure—it was how she connected. She built trust one conversation at a time, investing in people regardless of title or tenure. Her ability to drive results through genuine relationships set her apart. She didn't demand buy-in—she earned it. By listening, showing up, and making people feel seen, she turned teams into believers and vision into action. That's not just leadership—that's influence with integrity.

The 4S Framework—Support, Strive, Standards, and Success—is a direct reflection of the way she leads. It's born from real boardroom battles, culture shifts, and personal grit. This isn't a leadership theory polished in isolation. It's a blueprint built from lived experience. Stacie's experience.

For those of us who've seen her in action, none of this comes as a surprise. We watched her move through doubt, break ceilings, and build something enduring in every market she touched. She led with heart and demanded excellence—of herself first, then of everyone around her.

In these pages, you'll find the roadmap to do the same. If you're leading through transition, carving your own lane, or simply trying to show up stronger when the odds are stacked—this playbook is for you. Not just to inspire, but to activate your leadership, sharpen your perspective, and remind you of the power you already carry.

Stacie rose. Not because she was handed a path, but because she forged one. And now she's handing you the torch.

Use it.

David Oliveira
SVP, Head of Consumer Sales
Fortune 500 Company

Introduction

The 4S Framework by Stacie Selise

I've sat at tables I once prayed to be at, and I've built tables when there were none.

My journey from entry-level to executive taught me that true leadership isn't about titles, it's about alignment, intentionality, and impact. And while I've led sales teams, turned around underperforming markets, and cultivated top-tier talent, the biggest transformation came when I began to lead from my own framework. One built not on fluff or theory, but lived experience, high standards, and radical accountability.

That's where The 4S Framework was born.

Support. Strive. Standards. Success.

These four pillars became my foundation for team culture, personal growth, and long-term legacy. I designed this playbook to give you not just language, but tools. Not just insight, but application. This is for the leader who knows there's more. The one who's done things the "right" way and is ready to do it the aligned way.

Whether you're a corporate powerhouse, an emerging entrepreneur, or someone navigating both worlds, I created this for you. This isn't just about leadership. This is about legacy.

Let's build yours.

CHAPTER 1:

What Is The 4S Framework?

"Leadership is not just about making moves, it's about making meaning."
— Stacie Selise

The 4S Framework by Stacie Selise isn't just another leadership model, it's a proven approach grounded in real results, real alignment, and real impact. Born from both boardroom strategy and people-first leadership, it shifts leaders from reactive to intentional, from transactional to transformational.

It is built on four distinct, powerful pillars:

Support

People First. Always.

Support is about how you show up for others, your team, your clients, your community, and how you build trust, inclusion, and collaboration into your leadership DNA. It's not soft, it's strategic. When people feel supported, they perform at their highest level.

You can't lead people you don't value. You can't grow people you don't understand.

Strive

Excellence Requires Motion.

Strive means you don't settle. Leaders who strive push boundaries, embrace growth, and pursue mastery, not perfection. This pillar is about your hunger, your resilience, and your drive to become better than you were yesterday.

Striving is the difference between a leader with a title and a leader with a purpose.

Standards

Set the Bar. Then Raise It.

Standards are your non-negotiables. They define your reputation, your work ethic, and your boundaries. As a leader, the standards you uphold shape the culture around you. It's not just about what you allow, but what you expect, what you teach, and what you tolerate.

Your standards shape your results more than your intentions ever will.

Success

Results that Reflect Your Power.

Success is more than performance metrics, it's about alignment, impact, and intentional outcomes. This pillar teaches you to define what success looks like for *you* and your team, then build toward it unapologetically.

We're not chasing success, we're leading it.

Why This Framework Matters

While most leadership models focus on what to *do*, The 4S Framework by Stacie Selise™ focuses on how to *be*. Because your presence, your decisions, and your standards shape the outcomes long before a strategy is executed.

This isn't about theory. It's about Power. Presence. Precision.

And most of all, legacy.

CHAPTER 2:

Leadership & Legacy

From Influence to Impact

There comes a moment when every real leader realizes that their influence reaches far beyond performance metrics. It's not just about the numbers. It's about people. Lives. Energy. Futures.

That moment came for me when I understood that I wasn't just coaching people to hit targets, I was playing a real part in their livelihood. I was helping someone buy their first home. Helping someone get out of debt. Watching someone walk into their first apartment with pride. Those are the things that hit me as a leader. I wasn't managing a group of employees. I was guiding people who had goals for themselves, their families, and their future.

I realized I could be the reason someone went home at night and said, "I can't stand my job," or "I love what I do and who I work with." That level of responsibility changes everything. That is when I knew I wasn't just a manager, I was a leader.

The difference is clear. Managers oversee processes, Leaders carry people. And I chose to lead in a way that always puts people first.

What Legacy Really Means to Me

Legacy is not a buzzword. It's a thumbprint. It's what you leave behind when your name is no longer on the door, and your email is no longer in the system.

Every time I stepped into a new city or region, whether in New York, Connecticut, North Carolina, or Chicago, I knew my job wasn't just to drive results. It was to leave a mark. A culture. A tone. A feeling. I wanted teams to feel my leadership long after I was gone. That's what legacy looks like to me. Not just what I accomplished, but what I made possible for others.

When They Didn't Expect Me to Lead

In April 2021, I had just taken over as the Consumer Director for a large telecommunications company, leading the Chicago and Northern Indiana market. While the world was still grappling with the long-term impact of George Floyd's murder in 2020, new waves of civil unrest were rising after the fatal police-involved shootings of Daunte Wright and Adam Toledo. Tensions were especially high in Chicago, and downtown was expected to be one of the first areas to see a public response.

I was the newly promoted leader. There were people who didn't think I would know how to lead through something so complex. What they didn't realize is that I'm from New York City. I'm used to pressure. I'm used to having to move quickly, lead decisively, and take care of people in high-stakes moments.

When it became clear that stores near the heart of the city could be at risk, I gathered the data and made the call. We closed operations in advance, kept our teams off-site, and made sure every single employee was accounted for and safe. That's what real leadership is. You move with facts. You lead with compassion. And you never forget that your people are not just workers, they're human beings with families and loved ones who want them to come home safe and whole.

I did what I knew had to be done, and I did it quickly. That decision protected my team. And it proved that I was built for this.

The Culture That Lives On

One of my favorite legacies started when I was newly promoted in Southwest Connecticut. I began hosting team-building sessions that felt completely different. We didn't just gather for typical meetings. I brought in DJs. We held sessions after stores closed or before they opened. I gamified everything from sales to customer experience to store readiness.

We brought in energy, fun, and real learning. It wasn't just about hitting numbers. It was about creating a space where people could grow, connect, and actually enjoy the process. That culture still exists in some way today, even if my name isn't mentioned. And I'm okay with that. I know the spark I lit.

What This Chapter Teaches You

- Leadership is about responsibility, not just direction.

- Legacy is what stays after you leave.

- When people count you out, that's your opportunity to lead even louder.

- Culture isn't created in policy. It's created in how you make people feel.

JOURNAL PROMPT:
Leaving Your Mark

Take a few minutes to reflect and write:

✦ What's one moment that made you realize you were more than a manager or team lead?

_____

_____

_____

_____

✦ If you left your current role tomorrow, what would stay because of you?

_____

_____

_____

_____

✦ What legacy do you want to be known for, both personally and professionally?

_____

_____

_____

_____

CHAPTER 3:

The Powerhouse Leader

Presence. Purpose. Precision.

Being a leader is one thing. Being a powerhouse is something else entirely.

Powerhouse leaders move differently. They know who they are, what they bring to the table, and how to command a room without saying a word. Their impact is felt through their consistency, their energy, and their ability to make people believe in something greater.

I've been called a lot of things throughout my career, but the one I carry with the most pride is this: a presence. Not just a title. Not just a performer. A true presence. Someone whose energy shifts the temperature of a team, a call, or a meeting just by showing up with intention.

This chapter is about what it really means to step into that kind of leadership. The kind that doesn't beg for validation. The kind that knows its worth and moves with strategy and conviction.

Power Is an Energy, Not Just a Skillset

It's not about how much you know. It's about how deeply you own who you are. Powerhouse leaders don't shrink to make others feel comfortable. They take up space and create room for others to do the same. They walk in with clarity and purpose, knowing they were called to lead, not just placed in a position.

There were times in my career when I didn't have all the answers, but I still showed up with presence. That presence was built on preparation, consistency, and a deep belief in the work I was doing. When you show up prepared, your presence speaks before you do.

Three Qualities That Define a Powerhouse Leader

- **Clarity**

  You cannot lead well if you don't know who you are. Powerhouse leaders have clarity around their purpose, their values, and their mission. They are not confused by trends, titles, or noise. They know why they're in the room.

- **Conviction**

  Leadership comes with moments of pressure, discomfort, and opposition. A powerhouse doesn't fold. They lead with conviction, even when their decisions are questioned. Conviction is not about being right. It's about being rooted.

- **Culture Creation**

  Powerhouse leaders are not just focused on performance. They are focused on how people feel. They are builders of culture, protectors of energy, and architects of experience. They understand that results are tied to how people feel while they're getting there.

The Misunderstanding of Power

Power is often misunderstood. People think it's about being loud, being right, or being aggressive. But the most powerful people I've ever met know how to move in silence, lead without ego, and influence with intention.

As a Black woman in leadership, I've had to balance being seen and not being stereotyped. Being strong while still being soft. And what I've learned is that my power is not up for debate. I do not need to shrink for anyone, and neither do you.

The moment you realize you are the table, not just a guest at it, is the moment you start leading like a powerhouse.

What This Chapter Teaches You

- Power is not about perfection. It is about presence.
- You don't need a title to command respect. You need clarity, consistency, and confidence.
- Culture is one of the most powerful tools a leader can shape.
- Being a powerhouse is not a performance; it's an alignment.

JOURNAL PROMPT:
Defining Your Power

Reflect on these questions:

✦ When was the last time you truly felt powerful in your role? What were you doing?

_____

_____

_____

_____

✦ What qualities do you carry that make you a powerhouse?

_____

_____

_____

_____

✦ How do you want people to feel when they experience your leadership?

_____

_____

_____

_____

✦ What part of your leadership needs more ownership or alignment to feel like the powerhouse version of you?

_____

_____

_____

_____

CHAPTER 4:

Activating Support

Creating the Space for People to Rise

Support is not a soft skill. It's a leadership standard. It is the foundation for everything else that follows. When people feel supported, they show up differently. They take risks. They speak up. They lead stronger. The environments we create as leaders can either make people feel safe to rise or afraid to move.

To me, support means building psychological safety. That means people feel safe enough to speak up without fear of retaliation or shame. It means they feel seen as human first, not just as a role or number. When someone on your team is comfortable asking for help or being honest about what they need, you know support is in place.

I used to tell my team, "I don't have an open-door policy. Navigate as if there is no door." Because support isn't about having a door open. It's about never creating barriers in the first place. In my earlier leadership days, you could barely find me in my office. I wasn't sitting behind a desk waiting for things to go wrong. I was on the floor, with the team, present and visible. That was my way of saying, "I'm in this with you." And that presence mattered.

Even as I grew in the organization and took on more senior-level roles, I never lost that mindset. When I needed to close the door for a conference call or confidential conversation, I did. But as much as possible, I led without walls. That's what support looks like in action.

Support Is Human. Not Just Helpful.

Support also shows up in the hard moments. I've had team members lose loved ones. And yes, we made sure they could take their bereavement time without question. But we went further.

One of the most thoughtful things we did as a team was to send weekly groceries or pre-prepared meals to the homes of employees during their grieving period.

There's a service that allows you to send essentials for a week, so the person doesn't have to worry about what to cook or shop for. When you're grieving, the last thing you're thinking about is what's for dinner. Being able to remove that burden gave our team members the space to rest, heal, and feel supported in a way they never expected.

It wasn't just about being nice. It was about leading with intention. It was about seeing the human being, not just the employee.

When Support Is Missing

I've also had leaders who did the opposite. They made me feel small. They were dismissive, rude, and in some cases even vindictive. Some were biased and carried that bias into their decisions and treatment. And yes, it left a mark. But I don't regret those experiences. They taught me exactly what kind of leader I never wanted to be.

The truth is, there are two types of leaders who shape you: the ones who inspire you to rise, and the ones who show you what to avoid. Both are necessary. Both are powerful. And I am who I am because I experienced both.

Support Takes Emotional Intelligence

When I coach or meet with team members one-on-one, I always bring the human element. Yes, we review performance. Yes, we look at metrics. But I also check in on the person behind the results. How are they doing? What might be going on at home? What are they carrying that might be showing up in their work?

Leadership without emotional intelligence is just management. True leadership asks deeper questions. It makes space for vulnerability. It creates the conditions for people to bring their full selves to the table.

Sometimes a performance dip isn't about capability. Sometimes it's about life. And if you're not asking the right questions or creating space for the truth, you'll miss the chance to lead the person, not just the role.

Support Is a Collaboration

I have never believed in top-down leadership. When someone is struggling or facing a challenge, I don't walk in with all the answers. Rather, I ask, "What do you think we can do to get from here to there?" Then I follow up with, "What do you need from me?"

When people have a say in the solution, they are more likely to own the outcome. That's support in motion. That's leadership that builds leaders.

What I Hope They Say About Me

If you asked anyone who's ever worked with me, I would want them to say I was a strong leader who knew how to drive results. But I would also want them to say I made it fun. That I created a culture where people felt safe. That I challenged them, celebrated them, and supported them like they mattered. Because they did.

We were never just focused on individual glory. We played for the name on the front of the jersey, not the back. We knew that collective strength beats isolated wins every time. And when everyone feels supported, everyone has a reason to show up as their best self.

What This Chapter Teaches You

- Support starts with presence, not performance.

- Creating psychological safety is a leadership responsibility.

- Emotional intelligence is the foundation of trust.

- People do their best work when they know they are not doing it alone.

- Great leaders ask, listen, and co-create solutions.

JOURNAL PROMPT:
Leading with Support

Take a few minutes to reflect on the following:

✦ How do you currently show support to the people around you?

_____

_____

_____

_____

✦ What kind of support do you wish someone had given you earlier in your career?

_____

_____

_____

_____

✦ Do your team members feel safe being honest with you? Why or why not?

_____

_____

_____

_____

✦ What is one way you can intentionally lead with more support this week?

_____

_____

_____

_____

CHAPTER 5:

Living the Strive Mindset

Excellence in Motion

S triving is the pursuit of excellence, even when perfection isn't the goal. I've always believed that while perfection may not exist, if you strive for excellence, you'll land somewhere in the ballpark of perfection every time. That's what matters. Not flawless execution, but a heart-led commitment to give it your all.

Striving is not just hard work. It's heart work. I used to say this to my teams all the time. It's not only about checking boxes or doing what's required. It's about leading with passion, showing up with intention, and keeping your purpose front and center. Your heart has to be in it. Because when it is, the results speak for themselves.

When you lead with heart and push for excellence, it changes how your team shows up. It sets the tone for the culture. People don't just work harder. They work with pride, ownership, and a sense of meaning. That's the strive mindset.

Proving the Doubters Wrong

There were times in my career when people doubted I could succeed outside of the Northeast, where I built my name and reputation. When I moved to the Southeast, there was this quiet assumption that I wouldn't be able to adapt. That I wouldn't connect with a new market. That I wouldn't be able to win without the environment I'd always known.

But I knew who I was. I knew my leadership style. And I knew what I brought to the table.

I built strong relationships in that market, led with intention, and poured into my team. Not long after, we won a major mid-year leadership award. Although that award was for the team, it was also a reminder to the outside world. You can place me anywhere, and I will rise. Not because of location, but because of how I lead.

Later, when I moved to Chicago and Northern Indiana, I heard it again. "She'll never outperform what she did in New York." But once again, we proved them wrong. We stood toe to toe with one of the best territories in the nation. Our performance spoke for itself.

Every step, every move, every win, I strived to show that I could show up strong anywhere. And I did.

When They Tell You to Slow Down

As a young Black woman moving up through corporate leadership, I heard the same thing over and over again.

"Slow down."

"Be grateful."

"Where else do you expect to go after this?"

But here's what they didn't understand: I wasn't striving to be recognized. I was striving because I knew I was built for more.

That same mindset is what led me to entrepreneurship. It's why I now run my own self-titled consulting brand and lead The Stacie Selise Group. I wasn't created to stop at someone else's definition of success. I wasn't created to move at someone else's pace.

So no, I didn't slow down. I kept going. I will always keep going. And if I ever come up against a glass ceiling, I'll break it.

Striving with Balance and Boundaries

One of the best pieces of advice I ever received from a leader was, "Be where your feet are."

That means when I'm at work, I'm fully present at work. When I'm at home, I'm fully present at home. That level of presence helps me protect both my peace and my power.

I live by my calendar. And that means *everything* goes on it. Nail appointments. Hair appointments. Spa days. Date nights. Workouts. Me time. If I can show up for meetings and deadlines, I can show up for myself the same way.

Striving does not mean sacrificing yourself in the process. It means pursuing excellence without abandoning your wellness. It means leading fiercely and resting intentionally. That's how I do it. And I make no apologies for that.

What Striving Looks Like for Black Women

Let's be honest. Striving hits different when you're a Black woman in leadership.

We are still navigating male-dominated industries. We are still outperforming while being under-recognized. And we are still working ten times harder to receive half the credit. The data tells the story. Black women are the most educated group in America, yet we remain one of the most overlooked when it comes to leadership advancement.

So when I talk about striving, I'm not just speaking from ambition, I'm speaking from experience. For Black women, striving is not just about success. It's about survival. It's about showing up strong, even when the space wasn't designed for you. It's about creating your own lane when no one opens the door.

That's why this pillar of The 4S Framework matters so deeply. Because striving isn't just what we do, it's who we are.

What This Chapter Teaches You

- Striving is not about perfection. It's about presence, passion, and progress.

- Doubt from others can't stop a leader who knows their value.

- Slowing down to satisfy someone else's comfort is not your assignment.

- Boundaries are a form of excellence. So is self-care.

- For Black women, striving often means carrying more and still showing up powerful.

JOURNAL PROMPT:
Living the Strive Mindset

Reflect on these questions here or in your journal:

✦ What does striving look like in your life
   right now?

_____

_____

_____

_____

✦ Where are you giving your all, and where are you
   holding back?

_____

_____

_____

_____

✦ Have you allowed someone else's doubt to shape your pace or your goals?

_____

_____

_____

_____

✦ What's one way you can strive with more heart this week?

_____

_____

_____

_____

CHAPTER 6:

Leading with Standards

The Bar Starts Here

Leadership is not just about setting goals. It's about setting standards. Goals are what we aim for. Standards are what we live by.

Having high standards means leading with integrity, consistency, and excellence. I used to tell my team all the time, "There's winning, and then there's winning the right way." I never wanted any asterisk next to our name. No shortcuts. No gray areas. Just clean wins, built on trust, ethics, and heart work.

When you lead with standards, you set the tone for everything. The way people show up. The way results are earned. The way the culture moves. It's not about micromanaging. It's about making sure everyone understands the difference between just doing the job and doing it at our level.

We Don't Just Meet the Bar. We Are the Bar.

Sales is competitive. One great year sets the expectation for the next. And when you're at the top, people expect you to stay there. I've always embraced that pressure because I knew the kind of leader I was. And I knew the kind of teams I built.

When we performed at a high level, I didn't let the energy die down. I raised the bar. I reminded the team, "We are the bar." I didn't want us to just hit the target. I wanted us to become the standard that others looked at and tried to match.

That mindset helped us stay number one. Not just because of the numbers, but because of how we moved. How we collaborated. How we carried ourselves. We weren't just delivering results; we were setting the tone.

Holding People Accountable with Purpose

There's a difference between being strict and being clear. I believe in clarity. That's why I coach consistently. I don't wait until things fall apart to step in. I believe in ongoing feedback because leadership is about helping people adjust in real time, not catching them after they've already failed.

But coaching only works when both sides are committed. I've had moments where I did everything I could: developed plans, provided tools, gave honest feedback, and someone still chose not to meet the standard. At that point, the accountability conversation had to happen.

When someone makes it clear they don't want to do the work or uphold the expectations we agreed on, it becomes a choice. Either they grow into the role or they grow out of it. I don't believe in surprises. I believe in structure, transparency, and giving people every opportunity to succeed. But if they opt out, I help them transition into something that's a better fit.

That's not cold. That's leadership with care and structure. That's what standards require.

My Non-Negotiables

Every leader should have a few lines they never cross. For me, it always comes down to two things: integrity and respect.

Integrity is doing the right thing even when no one is watching. That means being honest, accountable, and ethical regardless of pressure or performance. I always tell my team, "I will go hard for you. I will have your back in any situation. But if you operate without integrity, I can't protect you." That's the line.

Respect is about how we treat ourselves and others. It doesn't matter how smart or skilled you are. If you don't treat people well, you're not a leader in my eyes. We're adults. There's no excuse for disrespect whether it's toward your peers, your team, your customers, or your leaders.

If you violate either of these non-negotiables, we have a problem, because you're not just impacting results, you're compromising the culture.

Why Standards Matter

When standards are clear, the team aligns. Everyone knows what's expected. Everyone knows how to show up. It creates consistency. It creates trust. It creates a culture where accountability feels normal, not personal.

It also builds reputation. I've seen entire teams shift because of strong standards. Not just in performance, but in presence. The way they move. The way they show up in meetings. The way they speak about the brand. You know a strong team when you see one. And more often than not, it's because someone took the time to set the tone and hold the standard.

What This Chapter Teaches You

- Standards are the backbone of leadership.
- Integrity and respect should never be negotiable.
- Coaching must be ongoing, not just corrective.
- Accountability is a process rooted in clarity and care.
- When standards are high and consistent, the culture will follow.

JOURNAL PROMPT:
Holding the Standard

Reflect on the following:

✦ What are your top two non-negotiables as a
leader or professional?

_____

_____

_____

_____

✦ Have you communicated your standards clearly
to the people around you?

_____

_____

_____

_____

✦ Are there areas where you've been too lenient
and it has affected your team or business?

_____

_____

_____

_____

✦ What's one standard you want to reinforce moving forward?

_____

_____

_____

_____

CHAPTER 7:

Defining Success on Your Terms

Redefining What Winning Really Means

Success used to be something I chased based on someone else's definition. Someone else's title structure. Someone else's goals. Someone else's idea of what a "win" should look like.

Now, success looks and feels completely different. It's about alignment. It's about impact. It's about being able to live life and lead work on my terms.

I'm no longer trying to meet standards set by systems that were never designed with me in mind. I've created my own. And when I build from a place of heart, purpose, and vision, I always land where I need to be.

That is success.

The Shift

For years, I defined success by what the company decided mattered - performance targets, rankings, constantly moving goalposts.

Now, I lead my own business. I own the journey. I define what success looks like, and I get to build based on my lived experience and real testimony. No more proving myself to systems that shift the rules every time you get close.

This isn't theory. It's freedom. And it's earned.

The Most Aligned I've Ever Felt

The moment I felt most successful wasn't when I received a bonus or when my name landed at the top of a leaderboard. It was when I made the decision to walk away and bet on myself.

Starting my business, watching it come to life, and knowing that everything I do from this point forward is rooted in my purpose, that's real success. That's alignment.

Still, I won't discount the moments in my corporate career where I felt proud. One of those was earning a top 1 percent award in the telecommunications company I worked at, a prestigious honor that rarely includes both a senior director and two of their district managers. But we made it happen. We led with heart. And we earned that trip to Maui together as a team.

That moment was special. But it wasn't the destination. It was a chapter. And now, this one is mine.

Success Is Not Just the Scorecard

Results matter, but culture is what tells the real story. I always said I could walk into any one of my stores and *feel* whether leadership was present. The energy, the tone, the way people move, all of that speaks louder than numbers.

True success is in the growth of people. How many teammates have been promoted? How many found their voice or moved into a space that aligned with their purpose? How many lives were impacted simply because you showed up as a strong, intentional leader?

That's the real metric.

It's not just about making money, it's about making leaders.

The 4S Connection

Success is the outcome of the first three pillars.

> If you've created Support
>
> If you've committed to Strive
>
> If you've upheld your Standards

Success will follow.

It's not a secret, it's a strategy.

And when you align your values with your work, you stop chasing success and start *leading* it.

What This Chapter Teaches You

- Success is not one-size-fits-all. It should reflect who you are and what you value.

- Alignment is more powerful than approval.

- Growth, culture, and elevation are key success indicators.

- You can walk away from one version of success and build a better one.

- The 4S Framework creates the foundation for long-term, sustainable success.

JOURNAL PROMPT:
Your Definition of Success

Reflect and write:

✦ What does success look like for you right now, based on *your* terms?

_____

_____

_____

_____

✦ What was your definition of success that no longer aligns with your purpose?

_____

_____

_____

_____

✦ How are you measuring success beyond results?

_____

_____

_____

_____

✦ What's one outcome, cultural shift, or growth story that lets you know you're leading well?

_____

_____

_____

_____

FINAL RECAP:

Make The 4S Framework Work for You

The 4S Framework was created from lived experience, hard lessons, and undeniable wins. It was born through the journey of rising through corporate leadership as a Black woman, stepping into entrepreneurship, and creating a path that didn't always exist before I walked it.

This framework is not just a leadership model, it's a set of guiding principles you can carry into every chapter of your life, whether you're leading a team, launching a business, navigating a transition, or figuring things out as you go. The 4S Framework is here to support you, challenge you, and remind you of the power you already carry.

Let's recap what each "S" is meant to unlock:

Support

Lead with presence. Create space for others to rise. Build with empathy, honesty, and real connection.

Strive

Pursue excellence with heart. Let your passion drive your progress. Push forward, even when the world tells you to pause.

Standards

Hold the line. Set the tone. Choose integrity and clarity over popularity. Protect the culture you're building.

Success

Define it for yourself. Build it on your terms. Let your impact, not just your outcomes, be the true measure of your legacy.

This framework is here for you. Use it. Apply it. Make it your own. Because when you lead with the The 4S Framework mindset, you create results that last and a reputation that speaks before you ever say a word.

A Final Message from Stacie

To the leader who feels unseen, stuck, or unsure, keep going.

Keep striving for excellence in all that you do. Even in moments where it feels like no one is watching or everything is unclear, I want you to remember this: there are peaks and there are valleys. The peaks will feel powerful, but it is the valleys that mature you.

The journey is the destination.

Every lesson. Every delay. Every breakthrough. It is all shaping you for what's next.

You are not alone. And you are not done.

You've Got the Framework. Now Use It.

Your story matters. Your impact is coming. And I can't wait to see how you lead from here.

With power and purpose,

Stacie Selise

Toolkit & Resources

Your Companion for Applying The 4S Framework by Stacie Selise

This isn't just a framework to *read,* it's a system to *live by.* The tools in this section will help you take action, reflect with intention, and stay aligned with the version of success that belongs to *you.*

Print them. Save them. Revisit them as often as you need to.

1. The 4S Weekly Check-In Template

Every Sunday or Monday, ask yourself:

- **Support:** Who do I need to support this week? Where do I need support myself?

- **Strive:** What's one thing I'm striving to improve or elevate?

- **Standards:** Where have I let my standards slip? How will I course correct?

- **Success:** What will success look like by the end of this week?

2. Powerhouse Leadership Self-Assessment

Rate yourself from 1–5 in each area below
(1 = needs focus, 5 = leading strong).

Reassess monthly.

- I create psychological safety on my team

- I model and reward striving for excellence

- I clearly communicate expectations and hold my standards

- I celebrate aligned wins and define success on my terms

- I manage my energy, not just my time

- I lead with presence, even under pressure

Reflection:

✦ What's one area I'm proud of right now?

_____

_____

_____

_____

✦ What's one area I will elevate in the
    next 30 days?

_____

_____

_____

_____

3. The 4S Culture Snapshot (For Teams)

Use this with your leadership team or direct reports to shape conversation around team dynamics.

As a team,

- Do we support one another or work in silos?

- Are we striving, or just surviving?

- What's the standard around here and who's setting it?

- How do we define success beyond the numbers?

This can be a great conversation starter during team huddles, skip-level meetings, or leadership offsites.

4. Leadership Values Clarifier

Use this to align your personal leadership identity with your actions.

✦ Three words that describe how I want to lead:

_____

_____

_____

✦ Three words that describe how I currently lead:

_____

_____

_____

✦ Where is the gap? What's one way I will close it this month?

_____

_____

_____

_____

5. Resources & Ongoing Support

If this playbook spoke to you, I would love for you to stay connected and become part of the movement.

- **Visit** www.stacieselise.com

- **Book a one-on-one Power Session here:** www.stacieselise.com/power-session

- **Subscribe** to the Stacie Selise Vault newsletter for exclusive leadership tools, behind-the-scenes access, updates, events, and invitations to join the community. Sign up here: www.stacieselise.com/ (The stay connected form)

- **Follow me on all social platforms** *@stacieselise*

- **Tag me directly or use the #The4SFramework hashtag** to let me know how you're applying The 4S Framework in your own journey. I want to hear from you.

BONUS:
The 4S Framework Manifesto

Print this. Post this. Live this.

- **I lead with Support.**
  I build people, not just processes.
  I create space for others to rise.

- **I Strive for Excellence.**
  I give it my all. I work with heart. I never settle.

- **I protect my Standards.**
  I move with integrity. I lead with clarity. I
  hold the bar.

- **I define Success for myself.**
  I don't chase titles. I create impact. I lead with
  alignment.

- **This is The 4S Framework by Stacie Selise™.**
  And I live it every day.

About the Author

Stacie Selise is a dynamic executive leadership strategist, speaker, and founder who has redefined what it means to lead with clarity, culture, and presence.

Her leadership journey began on the frontlines and evolved into a top-performing executive role at a Fortune 20 company, where she led some of the most competitive markets in the country. With more than a decade of experience in sales, customer experience, and organizational culture, Stacie has built her career on real results, high standards, and unwavering integrity.

As the creator of The 4S Framework by Stacie Selise™, she brings a human-first approach to leadership that blends strategy, heart, and measurable impact. Her framework serves as the foundation for her dual-impact brands:

- **The Stacie Selise Group:** A leadership and business development firm focused on empowering women professionals and advancing organizational culture. Through workshops, strategy, and executive development, The Stacie Selise Group partners with corporations and institutions to elevate women leaders and build more inclusive, high-performing teams.

- **Stacie Selise (Self-Titled Brand):** A high-level consulting and thought leadership platform where Stacie speaks, coaches, and collaborates with professionals, founders, and organizations ready to grow with intention, strategy, and impact.

Together, these brands reflect her vision, her voice, and her mission to help others lead with excellence and build their own version of success.

**To learn more, visit *www.stacieselise.com*
Follow @stacieselise on all platforms**

www.ingramcontent.com/pod-product-compliance
Lightning Source LLC
Chambersburg PA
CBHW070350130626
46556CB00007B/3105